SPIRITUAL NOTES
to MYSELF

Essential Wisdom
for the 21ˢᵗ Century

HUGH PRATHER

CONARI PRESS
Berkeley, California

Conari Press books are distributed by Publishers Group West

ISBN: 1-57324-113-X

Cover art direction: Ame Beanland
Cover photograph by: Toshio Nakajima; courtesy of Photonica
Designed and electronically produced by: Suzanne Albertson
Interior illustrations: Suzanne Albertson

Library of Congress Cataloging-in-Publication Data

Prather, Hugh
    Spiritual notes to myself : essential wisdom for the 21st century /
Hugh Prather.
        p.   cm.
    ISBN 1-57324-113-X (trade paper)
    1. Conduct of life.   2. Spiritual life.   I. Title.
BF637.C5P8   1998
291.'32—dc21   97-35032
                                                         CIP

Printed in the United States of America on recycled paper
10 9 8 7 6 5 4 3 2 1

More Praise for
Spiritual Notes to Myself

"We all need to converse with spirit. It is the only true guide we have. Read and then start taking notes."

—Bernie Siegel, M.D., author of *Love, Medicine and Miracles*

"Reading Hugh Prather is like experiencing a warm shower running inside of you."

—Wayne W. Dyer, author of *Your Sacred Self*

"An inspirational reminder and guide that the numinous is always alive within the human spirit."

—Angeles Arrien, Ph.D., author of *The Four-Fold Way*

"A small book of miracles... Every page speaks with quiet wisdom, offering gentle guidance for life's daily challenges. Most important of all, the author's words remind us how to listen for the clear voice of our own higher self!"

—Hal Zina Bennett, author of *Follow Your Bliss*

"Picking up this new book by Hugh Prather is like taking the hand of a good Friend... a Friend who can lead us 'Home,' to the truth of our real Purpose here."

—Joan Walsh Anglund, author of *A Friend Is Someone Who Likes You*

"Hugh Prather offers us thoughtful answers and patient insights. The wit and wisdom in this book are brief and to the point and yet deeply intuitive—like fortune cookies for the soul!"

—Beverly Hutchinson, Founder/Director of Miracle Distribution Center

"I have written *WOW!* throughout this book. It is filled with the simple Truths of God and with inspiring and practical material for living."

—Dr. David Wilkinson, United Methodist minister and a leader in the Reconciling Congregation Movement

"Our spiritual efforts do not give us privileges in the world—no parking places that manifest magically, no fat bank accounts. Hugh says it up front and straight out. What readers of this intimate notebook will discover, however, is how Truth reveals itself through the ordinary, daily experiences of our lives—if we choose to live consciously."

—Patricia Hopkins, co-author of *The Feminine Face of God*

"This book is powerful! Hugh's writing is insightful, gentle, fun and right on the money. Whatever you are experiencing in life's journey, *Spiritual Notes to Myself* will definitely help you work through it. Now Hugh Prather has written two classics that will live forever."

—Wally Amos, keynote speaker

"The most potent spiritual guidance I know....It offers deeply practical and clear instruction in how to walk with God—daily, one step at a time. A timely and gentle wake-up call to all that is truly healing and holy."

—Rubin R. Naiman, Ph.D., Director, The Little Temple, Community Healing Arts Institute, Tucson

to Gayle and our boys

*—who wrote this book so deeply in
my heart that all I had to do was
transcribe it*

Why Now?

In the late 1960s I wrote a book entitled *Notes to Myself*, which was published in 1970. I look back on it now as a writing that in some ways transcended its time but in many ways did not. Certainly we have all learned much since those days of self-examination, self-fulfillment, self-expression, and numerous other focuses on the individual or separate self. It was a time when even the word "selfishness" went from a negative to a positive. As a society, we still are cleaning up many loose ends from that period. In the groups my wife Gayle and I run for couples and parents, we continue to see individuals tenaciously holding on to myths such as "You have to give to yourself before you will have anything to give to others" and "You can't make someone else happy; you can only make yourself happy" and maybe the saddest of all: "As parents we have to reclaim our rights; we are not our children's servants." Ironically, it is now two thousand years since Jesus said, "Who is greater, the one at the table or the one who serves? Surely, the one at the table. Yet here I am among you as one who serves."

To some extent, *Notes to Myself* suffered from this type of preoccupation with the unconnected or unserving self. It was based on the premise that we learn about ourselves by studying our private feelings, patterns, thoughts, "dreams," reactions to others, and so forth. I believed that by becoming more aware I could improve myself, the way I approached other people, and my life in general. My assumption was not so much wrong as it was incomplete. Certainly it's a good thing to look in our hearts and see what we believe. We all have layers of feelings that become more loving and unifying the deeper we go into them. But at the time, I still was thinking that I was made equally of love and fear, driven equally by the desire to heal and the desire to hurt. I saw the distinction, but I identified with both. This makes for a very slow journey. Today I see more clearly the great gulf between the little self or "ego" and the united or "deeper self."

The 1970s marked the emergence of a general preoccupation with ego enhancement. We had sensitivity groups, consciousness-raising groups, encounter groups, and the beginnings of a tide of books and speakers urging us to love ourselves and "honor" our feelings. Although this movement did much good, its prominent feature was the ideal that, above all, we should define our ego's needs and devote ourselves to meeting them. Indeed, our ego's needs should not operate unconsciously, but when meeting them is our primary focus in life, we become preoccupied with all we haven't been getting and must get now. This attitude is quite separating and not at all as "empowering" as it is commonly believed to be.

Within us is a source of power that is far greater than our separate feelings, separate opinions, and separate agendas: our unity with other people. A selfish person is like a single power line attached to nothing. Making the line fatter and longer is impressive but accomplishes nothing. If we devote ourselves to our private differences, we journey down a dead-end road toward loneliness and loss. Far too many people today are ending their lives with a list of petty victories and meaningless gratifications that no one cares about—because they themselves cared about no one. And yet, entreaties to our oneness are distrusted and disbelieved. To much of the world, they are at best a joke; at worst, dangerous rantings.

The thing I lacked most when I wrote *Notes to Myself* was the *experience* of what connects us. I gave lip service to the concept of oneness, but it was still mere philosophy, just one idea among many. In another early book I posed the question of whether there is another way to go through life "besides being pulled through it kicking and screaming." When I wrote that I was still in love with the question. Now I am in love with the answer.

But please understand, the answer does not lie in having to embrace Judaism, Buddhism, fundamentalism, Catholicism, or any other *ism*. Nor does it lie in mere belief in God. Believing is of limited use. Sacred scriptures and inspired writings can point the way, but finally you have to walk where they are pointing. This you can do with the aid of a system or by listening to the stillness within you. Either way is fine, but ultimately you must stop searching and simply do it.

There is a way to have a growing fulfillment, a deepening peace, and an unreasonable happiness free of circumstances and events. It lies in recognizing our oneness with all living things. To me God is what binds us together. This is another way of saying God is Love. We simply are not separate. We do not have little private thoughts that affect no one but ourselves. All of that is an illusion, albeit a powerful one. Yet it will remain the hard fact of life until we feel, experience, and immerse ourselves in the stream that runs through us all.

There is no evidence outside of us that this eternal, unchangeable stream exists. Yet we only seem to turn to this one thing our eyes can't see or judge when we have grown tired of the world's usual patterns and of our own small thoughts. I write this book because I assume that you, like me, now feel a yearning for a simpler life and for relationships that last. There is unquestionably a way for you to have the life you long for. I now know this beyond any doubt.

Clearly an ego is not all we are. Nor is the ego's puny range of experience all we believe in. Most individuals have had at least a moment when they felt joined with something greater than themselves. Perhaps they felt swept up in the strains of extraordinary music, or felt utter stillness before the magnificence of nature. Perhaps they experienced an instant of perfect love for a child or an animal and the joy they felt was beyond human description. Perhaps they sensed the existence of an order or a perfection and suddenly they knew that it included everything and everyone. Maybe there was no outward evidence of this perfection or order, but they had a deep knowing nonetheless. Others have felt the touch of God's peace at the very moment of tragedy or loss. Here the evidence before their eyes *refuted* what they felt, but somehow they sensed the unshakable grounds for that peace.

As the old hymn says, "My God is real . . . 'cause I can feel . . . Him in my soul." That experience is undeniable. It is more powerful and intimate than anything in the world. Just one instant of the knowledge of God destroys even the laws of physics. It brushes aside time and space. It brushes aside death. For within the peace of God we can feel the presence of a loved one who may be continents away, or that someone who has died and no longer "exists" in the world in any meaningful sense is now with us, a living presence we cannot lose.

However, you don't need an overwhelming spiritual experience to begin. Signs and wonders are nice but not required. In order to start, you don't even need to have your questions answered. All you need is the intent to start. In a sense, this book is the field notes of how one person began his journey. These are the things I have said to myself and to others when I was not qualifying my sentences or trying to sugarcoat the truth. They are the things that Gayle and I have been thinking and increasingly living for many years. Believe me, they are pretested! You can take them to the bank.

As I did in *Notes to Myself*, I have tried in this volume to select and arrange passages to form a whole. Study this little book and you will have at least one route to "the place of eternal beauty." Apply the ideas daily, and you will stay there. This promise would be arrogant except that "the way" is so simple that even little children instinctively know it. The secret they feel—the one that is always happily bubbling up within them—is that, actually, we never left that place. We just forgot where we are.

My use of "you"

Having boys who love team sports, Gayle and I frequently have seen them talk to themselves in the course of a game: "You're not watching the ball." "Get your head in the game." "Swing [the bat, club, racket] from your hips, not your arms." In the following notes, I frequently use the second person in a similar way—to get my own attention.

Although occasionally I do address "you" the reader, most often I am not being blunt with you, but with myself. A firm reminder can cut through my mental dawdling: "Forget what just happened [Hugh], and get back to what's important." In this sense, many of the notes in this book are more like ones I might tape to the bathroom mirror or refrigerator door, rather than the more tentative notes I would enter in a diary.

The mind can and should be self-correcting, and sometimes a healthy dose of mental firmness is an effective part of this process. However, in my opinion self-censure and guilt must never be an aspect of self-encouragement, because all forms of attack split the mind rather than unite and focus it.

Sometimes I get the feeling God has pets and I'm not one of them.

I have this notion that there's a plan or rhythm of the universe or divine guidance, and if I could just follow it, everything would turn out okay. The problem is it seems to be revealed in hidden signs and coded indicators—which, somehow, I'm supposed to read. No one hears, "Turn left at the next corner and there under a discarded burger wrapper will be the winning lottery ticket." So what do we really have here, a God who stands behind a room divider and mutters?

God is the only sane thing there is, and we are all a part of God. However, if I believe there's some divine law manifesting itself as parking places and fat bank accounts in the West, while allowing children in the East to step on land minds, I have got an insane God on my mind.

Jesus' life didn't go well. He didn't reach his earning potential. He didn't have the respect of his colleagues. His friends weren't loyal. His life wasn't long. He didn't meet his soul mate. And he wasn't understood by his mother. Yet I think I deserve all those things because I'm so spiritual.

We are walking in a ticker tape parade. That's all that's going on. Some pieces of confetti read "great calves," some "chronic sinus," some "no noticeable hair loss," some "multiple sclerosis," and some "third finger amputation." Don't judge your neighbor by what pieces of paper fall on his or her shoulders. Don't think you are cursed or "blessed" by what pieces fall on yours.

The fact is, nothing will go right today. And if it does, it will only scare you.

Are there miracles? Of course! But notice the effect of a miracle. It doesn't make us feel more separate and special, but more at one with all things. It's a mistake to think that God reveals the cure for my child's illness but not for yours, or even that God whispers the directions home into the ears of some lost pets but leaves others to perish.

A miracle isn't a detached event that I can talk about at the potluck. It doesn't smooth my way alone. It brings me a step closer to the place of stillness and beauty within me—and that smooths everyone's way.

If I had Bushwhacker Hot Sauce for dinner, no matter how I try to change the dream I'm having six hours later, it's just going to go bad again. It's the hot sauce. A disturbed dream is the product of a disturbed dreamer. And everyone who isn't fully awake is more or less disturbed. That's why the answer to all my questions is, "Wake up."

When I look back on some incident and ask, "Why did this happen? What does this mean?" I'm almost always thinking of something I have *already* classified as negative. I don't analyze the times I forgive or turn to God, or even analyze a favorable turn of events.

People who are unfaithful, "play hardball" in business deals with friends, win at any cost when competing in sports, or consistently leave inadequate tips are seldom tempted to ask "What does this mean?"

We say "It was meant to be" about the loss of a championship or about an untimely death. But we apply this explanation arbirtraily. We don't say this when athletes lose because a fan attacks them or when an infant dies in explosion.

There's this peculiar thought today that we "attract" negative experiences and relationships. And yet, no agreed-upon list of who or what is wholly negative exists. Even the darkest tragedies sometimes can lead to new understandings and strengths.

We can't control even the smallest event. However, we do choose what we experience. We decide to be awake to the stillness and peace of Love or to know merely the chaos of constant analysis and continual reinterpretation.

How the world strikes me is not precisely how it strikes *anyone* else. Even my own interpretations are unstable. Many past "defeats" I see now as past improvements, and many "victories" I see as spiritual failures. There are few if any aspects of my life that I am wise enough to change "for the better."

Although our take on other people and worldly circumstances differs, our experience of God, which is beyond the fumbling grasp of words, is universally the same.

God speaks to us in a thousand voices, each with the same clear message: "I love you. Please trust me on this one."

If your child is having a nightmare, you don't try to *perfect* the nightmare. If in her sleep she mutters, "Mommy, I'm a baby bird and the cat's about to get me," you don't say, "try hiding under a bush." That would just keep her dreaming. You kiss her on top of the head, sing her a song of comfort, and gently rock her awake. God is no less loving a parent than you.

Here I am moving from point A to point B to point C—in a fog. I turn to God and say, "How do I get to point D?" But God gently replies, "Take my hand and I will lead you out of the fog." Then I get stubborn and say, "You didn't answer my question!"

We ask God which apple we should buy, and think divine Love leaves the one with the rotten core for someone else. We may even think God saves one or two from the crash and leaves all the others to burn to death. We actually believe that what favors our *body* is a sign of God's grace.

God doesn't tell us where to get the shoes on sale or give us stock market tips. Don't even ask for that brand of advice. If you're getting a buy signal, you're hearing Edgar, The Higher Ego, not God.

Do I really think God doesn't know my question?

The answer is in my heart before I ask.

When my grandmother used to see me hopping up and down on one foot, she would say, "Hugh, just follow your little pee pee into the bathroom." And my grandmother was always right. Just follow your pee pee—your "peaceful preference," your deeper inclination toward simplicity. Forget what you want—bathe your mind in stillness—then notice that you have a peaceful preference, a gentle leaning in some direction. That's your answer.

Guidance isn't being told which action to take or not to take. Guidance is God's gift of peace—from which we proceed. The peace dissolves the question, and we simply do what we do in peace.

I *always* have a peaceful preference. But I have to be still enough to know it.

Following my peaceful preference doesn't assure me an outcome that my ego, or "little mind," will like. But it does join me with the source of peace, which is independent of assessments and interpretations.

My little mind is conflicted about what to do. And even after I have decided in peace, my little mind now is conflicted about the outcome.

Whether I grant someone's request because I'm fighting my ego or refuse to grant it because I'm giving in to my ego, I still am not connected to my real mind, my real feelings, my real identity.

The little mind always speaks first. For example, Gayle asks me to do something and immediately I feel resistance. I don't mind doing things, but I don't like to be asked. Now, don't fight that reaction. Wait an instant to let the deeper feelings come into focus. The impulses of the deeper self rise in stillness.

The ego is a fussy ol' geezer. It holds no peace. I know when my ego is speaking because I feel urgency or righteousness or excitement. "Do it before it's too late," says the ego. "It's better to be right than happy," says the ego.

The little mind thinks the choice is between two courses of action—eat the chocolate, don't eat the chocolate; tell the white lie, don't tell the white lie. But the only spiritually meaningful choice is between acting from peace or acting from conflict.

Our ego is the echo of the voices from our past. It's made up primarily of the influences and experiences we had during our formative years. These "lessons" combine to give us a sense of identity that is unrepresentative of our real, or peaceful, identity. Because the voices from our formative years disagree, our ego is deeply conflicted.

Within stillness I experience my peaceful mind, my united self. Obviously, stillness can't be attained by warring against a conflicted ego. That's why judging myself is as great a mistake as judging my neighbor.

The identity you think you are does not exist.

Our ego, or imaginary identity, functions very much like a child's imaginary playmate. Set up by the mind as separate and autonomous, it will defend itself. "Don't talk to the new kid on the block," the imaginary playmate says—because it knows that real friendship will dissolve it. Likewise, the ego counsels, "Don't consult your true feelings," because it knows that truth will dissolve it. But note that consulting what is true is not denouncing the ego. When children fight an imaginary friend, it takes stronger hold of their mind. But when they become interested in actual companionship, they lose interest naturally in imaginary companionship. Awakening is merely the arousing of our interest in our real self.

My mind shuttles between my inner spiritual efforts and the movie of my life that plays out before my eyes. Each time I turn to God, I quickly turn back to see if there's been any improvement in the script. Quite insanely, I am looking to my physical life for confirmation of my spiritual life! Somehow I think that because I try, people should behave and circumstance should shape up—and I am actually more interested in this than in God.

There is no reward in the world for our spiritual efforts. There isn't even a connection. The payoff for turning to God is more God, not more world.

If I tried to decide with love and with peace, if I did the best I could in that respect—but now I am second guessing and reconsidering what I decided—I am questioning a holy effort. Don't do that. Don't reconsider. Just keep walking in peace.

It's not that there is never a mistake or an evil motivation, but that there is something else as well. Forgiveness is the door to experiencing that something else.

Forgiveness doesn't excuse behavior; it looks past it to a greater truth.

The angels of heaven lay a path of peace before me. If I fall, I can fall only into God.

Our life unfolds as if God were showing us a slide show, and each slide is a little test. God says, "Can you forgive *this?*" If the answer is no, God simply moves the slide back for us to view again later.

We choose what we experience, not what we see. No matter what is happening—be it "good" or "bad"—say to yourself, "Even in this situation, I can believe in innocence; I can believe in peace."

Sometimes I'm afraid to forgive because I think I'll have to spend more time with the person—or make some other gesture. But forgiveness is an act of the heart, not a Kodak moment.

Forgiveness isn't something nice I do for someone who is "guilty." Forgiveness is something nice I do for my own *mind*. Do I want a mind that tortures me or one that is a friend to me?

The reason that judging splits my mind is that I am the neighbor I am condemning. "Love your neighbor as yourself" is a literal statement.

Judgment sticks labels on people. Forgiveness peels them off. God doesn't label; God sees. Only my *innocent* vision is 20/20.

Insight may tell me that someone is being dishonest right now— but judgment tells me that dishonesty is all there is to the person. The trouble with judgment is that it turns insight to concrete.

Forgiveness restores insight, and we *need* insight. It's our true vision. Insight looks at two cars and says, "*That* Ford will be more maintenance free than *that* Volvo." Judgment, however, doesn't see the two cars that are present. It says, "The Ford will be trouble because I *know* about Fords." If I can limit my ability to see a car, I certainly can limit my ability to see my child, spouse, or anyone else. My choice is to "know about" them or to see them in the present.

The reason I have nothing to fear from God is that God sees me.

Certainly we may be in pain from what someone did to us. Forgiveness doesn't ask us to deny the pain or to think dishonestly about the past. It asks us to look to God, where the wound has already been healed.

Forgiveness is the decision to out endure the ego. Therefore, don't try to forgive for all time; just forgive in the moment. Two minutes from now the grievance may come back. Simply forgive again in the moment. If you keep surrounding someone in light, soon your ego—which hates light—will stop handing you the grudge. That's because the ego is mere shadow and flees when you remember that you are the light of the world.

We think we must attack in order to act. We think we have to get angry to quit our job; we have to judge the congregation to change our house of worship; we have to build a case against our friend to step back from the relationship. If we get sick and shut the door to our room, we think we must shut the door to our heart as well.

Following a spiritual path is deciding that the picture before you will no longer dictate the orientation of your mind. If you must step back from a relationship, step forward with your mental absolution. If you must be sick, keep your loving thoughts around the people in your home. If you must die, leave not one living thing unblessed by your eternal presence.

Emotions are the new gods of our day. We discuss them endlessly. We form groups to elicit and dissect them. We abandon our family and friends because of them. We watch talk shows in which "How do you feel about what she just said?" is considered a profound question. Throughout the day we are vigilant for the tiniest shift in our emotions. If we feel a little tinge of sadness, everything comes to a halt. "What does it mean? What does it mean?" And yet our body's emotions tell us *nothing* about our Self, about God, or about the children of God.

The little mind is always feeling *something*. But I am called to address who I am, not how I feel.

The answer is not to ignore or deny my emotions. In fact, I must become more aware of them—but in a different way. Now I use awareness to take out the garbage.

It's fine to look at my past to see where some emotion or behavioral pattern is coming from. But this has limited healing benefits. The past can't be accurately reconstructed or interpreted. So it's pointless to ask what is "real." Instead, I must see all versions of the past that are in my mind and forgive each one. Then I am free to return to the truth that I have never left God's heart.

If we think we are only a body, then we think our emotions are our inner self. In that case we had better have some way of handling them so they don't go underground and control us unconsciously.

Tear up phone books; run and scream; pound on the mattress—do whatever is necessary to release what you believe is real. But don't vent your feelings on others, because that will only complicate your situation. It brings more people into the problem and will appear to take it out of your hands.

In all I do, let me be harmless. In all I do, let me take God's hand. I am not alone, even when dealing with my own mistakes.

One of the most spiritual songs ever written was "Keep Those Dogies Rollin'" from the TV series *Rawhide*. Now, you're probably not from Texas as I am, but I can tell you you don't want to tackle one of those young steers when they're rollin'. That's also the key to mental discipline—"keep them movin' along." The ego is a little cattle drive of thoughts that runs nonstop through the head. But tackle one of those thoughts and you've got yourself a problem, maybe even a stampede of emotion. Just let all the thoughts mosey on by.

Emotions are a by-product of some thought we've grabbed hold of. I don't care whether it's anger, ennui, fear, or whiny self-pity—the emotion is manufactured and packaged by the thought. Loosen the grip on the thought, and the emotion will begin to evaporate.

No matter what else I'm thinking, I also can think of God. That turns on a light. There is no contest between light and darkness. Literally, there is none. That's why there is nothing inside me I have to flee.

I didn't create my mind, so I don't have to battle it. Light is the function of the mind God made for me. Don't try to get rid of the thought, just add light to it. Where there is light, there is peace. Be peacefully irritated, peacefully depressed, peacefully jealous, peacefully frustrated, peacefully resentful. Pretty soon your whole being will be filled with light and you will be peacefully peaceful.

Say, "I drown in God and breathe in peace," and let your mind move past the words to the experience.

Let the mind of God descend over you, and disappear within it.

The ego *is* addicted. Within this part of my mind, I believe I am alone, so naturally the craving to unite with something else is enormous. The mistake I made was uniting with a harmful substance that had nothing to give. However, if I *remain* in my separate self after giving up the substance, my addictions merely shift.

The reason that transformations were so quick in the early days of Alcoholics Anonymous is that the "members" were clear that the aim of the program was to move from the mind that serves itself to the mind that serves others. The mind that serves others cannot be addicted. But if my focus is on strengthening and defining the separate self, I will never know the joy of the mind that serves.

Most idle thoughts are defensive. A conflicted mind is vulnerable and therefore fearful and suspicious. A victim mentality eventually seeks victims. It turns on itself and then on others. Only forgiveness unites the mind.

Be still and know that God is with you. A whole mind experiences the divine attitude. At home and at peace, it sings, and every person and each living thing becomes a note in one unending song.

Actions are not spiritual. I can "kill with kind-ness" and drive people up the wall with positive thinking.

"Finding something nice to say" about someone is not practicing love. If I tell a friend that the person who cheated him didn't mean it, I just make him feel more isolated and alone.

The world is a documentary of separation and nothing within it can prove Oneness. But we're not obliged to battle negative interpretations of the world with positive interpretations. Only when I turn to God can I see God.

Spirituality isn't an affectation. It isn't wearing white cotton and talking like a god. We can be spiritual without anyone knowing it. We can heal without anyone knowing it. We can awaken to Oneness without anyone knowing it. But if we start talking about our holiness—paint-ing a picture of how holy we are—we block our holiness.

Ducks quack and humans gossip. If you don't quack, the other ducks will run you off. If you don't gossip, you're going to have *very* short conversations.

My treasure is where my *heart* is. I don't need to be spiritually correct, but I do need to keep my heart in Love.

I can gossip without malice. I can complain about the government without resentment. I can rail against the weather without getting drenched.

When I am flexible and forgiving, I am happy. When I am rigid and righteous, I am unhappy. It's that simple.

To our ego, appearances are everything. Like flannel pajamas, the comfortable part is on the outside where it does no good. Likewise, our physical appearance and outward behavior are everything to the ego, while the thoughts behind our actions are of little concern. Yet in reality, we dwell in our mind, not in our actions. But the ego takes no real accounting of this. So we spend all this time in the morning trying to *look* prepared—getting the hair right, the clothes right—but we leave home with our minds in disarray.

On a spiritual path, the reverse is true: Form is secondary to content. So if I find myself preoccupied with the question of what to say or do, I am already caught up in the ego. Release the question and let God do the thinking. Now my actions can flow from oneness and peace, taking whatever form they take. There is no question about an action taken in peace. It *cannot* harm because peace accompanies it.

As a young boy I used to go to Mrs. Fulton whenever I got sick. She would close her eyes and quietly pray:

> *I am one with Thee,*
> *Oh Thou infinite one.*
> *I am where Thou art.*
> *I am what Thou art.*
> *I am because Thou art.*

And each time I would be healed. As an adolescent I started going to her with tortuous metaphysical questions. Mrs. Fulton would simply close her eyes and repeat the same prayer—and I would be healed of the question. I wouldn't even remember it as I left her apartment, carried along as if by angels.

There are no questions in God.

The key to good friendships is for me to enjoy my friends. The key to being a great parent is to enjoy my boys. The key to a sound marriage is to enjoy Gayle. And the key to walking a spiritual path is to enjoy my Self.

Beneath the garments of the world is joy.

A miracle is a gift of light, not a gift of worldly goodies. It shines *through* the world I see. Each new crack in the scenery tells me there is something else going on behind this play I think I'm in.

As Joel Goldsmith said, "The trouble with healing is that you don't know who you're putting back on the streets." Always heal the heart, and let the body tell its own story.

If I hold someone in my heart and heal my *own* heart, there's unquestionably the possibility of physical healing. But God doesn't enter into this process in some arbitrary way, withholding a blessing here, giving it there. We don't need a healing to be healed. Healing is *never* absent from God, and God is never absent.

Let no one pass me by unhealed—not one homeless person, not one damaged child, not one tailgater, not one angry clerk. Let me correct any thought or image that does not mirror God's all-encompassing love.

The only powers worth having, everyone already has. Practice healing and you will become a healer.

It's okay to offer physical healing as a symbol of love. And it's okay to offer chicken soup. But don't for a minute believe God heals some people and not others, or you're going to end up thinking God makes chicken soup, and that's going to tick off a lot of vegetarians.

Jesus didn't bless just his friends and family. When we *pray* for our daughter or son to win the game, we've missed the whole point of prayer.

When I've lost all interest in controlling out-
comes, I finally will be free to love everyone my
mind rest upon.

One man drinks beer, watches television, wildly
cheers for his team at games, and sometimes
says, "Pull my finger." Another man reads books,
attends meetings on spiritual subjects, and at
games, takes no sides. We say the second man is
more spiritual than the first. Yet the first man
may be a very loving father, a devoted spouse,
and a good friend, whereas the second man may
be righteous, rigid, and uncaring. We all know
relationships in which one partner attends the
meetings and talks the talk, and yet his or her
"spiritually illiterate" partner clearly is a better
human being. Even most little kids are better
human beings than the adults around them—
and young children can't even *grasp* a spiritual
concept!

As we awake, our actions will change. But we can't awake by changing our actions.

The mind receives the wholeness of God's love, but the *body* parcels it out. Thus I have no "right" to be stingy. I must be supportive of Gayle, our children, and others to whom I am important. I must sympathize with their losses and celebrate their victories. I must not kill their happiness in the name of "honesty."

Don't give "feedback." Give truth. The fact is that most people really are asking if they are wonderful, and my truth-filled answer is YES! Each of God's children is cherished and beloved. Even though I know in my heart and prayers that truth doesn't play favorites, *I* am dealing with one person at a time.

"I must be honest." "I must be true to myself." These words are almost always a preamble to a speech of abandonment or betrayal.

"I want to let you know how I've been feeling." But God is Love. To be what we were created to be, we don't always have to give an update on our negative emotions.

The reason it isn't helpful to go around talking about our healings, visions, and other spiritual fireworks is that such conversations tend to be separating and unloving. The little mind gets involved, we start feeling special, and the other person thinks he wasn't invited to God's party.

It should be obvious that the evidence of love, unity, and wholeness in our lives will begin to disappear whenever we choose to be special and separate.

The saints of God dare to be ordinary.

If we can see our oneness with just one other person, we become the light of the world.

A circle of wholeness is made up of two *opposite* halves. That is why the ark of love is entered two by two.

We are not always attracted to the "wrong" person. Unless something very unusual is going on, we are always attracted to an ideal healing partner. Do you think it's just bad luck that one of you likes to plan and one of you likes to be spontaneous? That one of you likes to talk it out and one of you likes to "let it be"? That one of you likes to spend and one of you likes to save? That one of you likes to party and one of you is more a homebody?

If you've got someone who seems opposite to you in almost every respect, you've got the right person. In a sense, your partner is the repository of your rejected strengths. Forgive your partner and, together, you become whole.

The old marriage vows had it right: We become one body. Our own body has a left side and a right side that cooperate. But it also has a center. Forgiveness gives marriage its center. Yes, at this time the two sides are fighting. But just hold faithfully to each other's innocence and you will become a complete spiritual body.

I will never succeed in truly changing another person. If I even want something from another person, I *will* succeed in becoming irritated.

Forget this doormat stuff. Jesus never did one single thing for himself. Was Jesus a doormat? Was he an enabler? Was he codependent? Did anyone ever yell, "Hey, Jesus! Get a life!"?

"I'm not responsible for you. I need my space, my boundaries, my beingness." Yes, I sometimes have those feelings, but because I am in a relationship, I also feel love, responsibility, and oneness.

If there's something in the eye, the whole body feels it.

You acknowledge your separate needs, and you meet them. But you help each other with this. Remember, you're married; you're one body now. If the nose itches, the hand scratches. The hand doesn't say, "It's your itch; it's your problem."

The question isn't whether to have arguments or to take time off to be by ourselves. The question is, what is our *intent* in arguing or withdrawing. I know couples who can strengthen their friendship by screaming at each other and storming around. But that's because they both are clear that the function of the ranting is to bring them closer together.

Today we say, "You can't make another person happy." But we sure can make our partners *angry*. We intuitively know exactly what to say or do. How is it we can make them upset, jealous, scared, and the like, but not happy? It is because we are in the habit of using our intuition negatively. Practice making your partner happy and you will become proficient.

Surely it's clear that relationships—whether with a child, friend, sibling, or spouse—crumble under pressure. If you want to make your partner happy, first you must stop being a source of pressure, demands, and ultimatums.

Many couples have noticed that when they have a day of closeness and peace, the next day is often a disaster. The ego merely is trying to recoup lost ground. We must learn to laugh gently at this. Our true relationship is a light that is replacing our separateness; and for a time, separateness seems to fight back.

Egos clash. That's the nature of egos. Treat these outbursts as sneezing fits. More harm is done analyzing them. Our spiritual relationship, not ego business-as-usual, deserves our preoccupation. When someone sneezes, we say, "God bless you." We don't say, "What exactly did you mean by that?"

Isn't it funny how during the honeymoon period, understanding each other is seldom a problem. "Communication skills" are highly overrated. We don't *want* to understand; that's the problem. We can't say to our dog or baby, "I want to give you a little feedback on something you've been doing lately," and yet we get along with them just fine. I know two couples who because of an accident and a stroke *can't* hear or talk but still are able to move past their problems and grow in love. Work on communicating better, but work also on dwelling in love, the place of true understanding.

There is a spiritual relationship that has no connection to the ego relationship. Ego love will die. But if we can gently establish ourselves within the spiritual relationship, it *will* outlast the end of the three and a half years of hormones, the fading of our bodies' blossoming periods, and the withering of age. And once we are in the spiritual relationship, even death can't touch our love. So every day, let us fall more deeply in love with each other's innocence. Within innocence we are already one.

Our puppy likes me to flip her on her back and scratch her tummy. Gayle wouldn't receive that as love. I must express love in a language that can be understood and appreciated by *that* person.

Don't ask yourself what *you* would like; don't even ask yourself what any reasonable person would like. Look at your spouse, your child, your friend, and *see* what they like. Loving your neighbor as yourself doesn't mean putting yourself in your neighbor's place. Leave your neighbors right where they are. You become *them*.

Sex has been removed from the *process* of life. Learning to read and write, mastering a trade, establishing a social life, bearing children, evolving a family routine, and developing a sex *life* once were all one process. Now each sexual encounter is analyzed, compared, and judged.

People with no real connection sometimes have great sex and people with a deep spiritual bond sometimes have poor sex. Sex simply is not the weather vane of the health of a relationship.

Sex has become a set of competing rights, with the emphasis on "What am I not getting?" The right to have our "needs met" competes with our partner's right not to be coerced. The right to foreplay competes with the right to reach orgasm. The right to experiment competes with the right not to feel vulnerable. The right to quality time afterwards competes with the right to get cleaned up or to sleep. Approached this way, we have no need for hell; sex provides it every time the subject comes up.

Of course one of you likes more sex or a different kind of sex than the other. Don't read anything into this. One of you also likes pizza more than mu shu pork—so what does *that* mean?

Divisions over sex have the same cause as all marital problems: something has been made more important than the relationship. Merely ask, "What can we do to build a deeper friendship between us?" "What can we do to restore this one little way of communicating to the same level of gentleness and forbearance we bring to other forms of communication?" and a hundred ways around the divisiveness will begin coming to mind.

Please God, let me remember that human relationships can withstand very little pressure. Yet somehow everyone thinks marriage is different. Because of the impossible expectations we have now that our partner should heal the past and fulfill our needs, marital relationships have become *more* fragile than common friendships!

Our primary relationship is a spiritual reality that exists apart from personalities. It needs to grow only in our awareness. But no living thing—including a relationship—can blossom in awareness when weighed down by expectations.

Make very few demands on your partner. If you can make none at all, that's best. Set up no tests and ask few questions. Don't try to cheer your partner up. Don't demand even that your partner stop being demanding!

Repeat in your heart, "I am wholly at peace with the way you are." Do this and your partner gradually will become your path to the peace of God.

If there's a question whether to say it, don't say it.

The tongue is very hard to control. If I feel an urge to bring something up that I know is likely to cause division between Gayle and me, I must pause long enough to become *completely* clear why I don't want to say it—or else I *will* end up saying it. And I *will* be sorry.

Rush to help your partner. But be intuitive about this. There is a difference between thinking you know what's best for your partner and sensing that your partner would welcome your help. As your oneness grows, your partner's pain will be your pain. You will experience it literally as yours. Then it will be your enormous pleasure to meet your partner's needs. This is the definition of a healer.

But what if your partner is violently insane? What if your partner is abusing your children? Or what if your partner is engaged in criminal activities? Then of course you immediately step away from the relationship. But in your mind, *never* lose faith in the seed of innocence God has placed within your partner.

The life that moves toward an innocent vision moves with increasing freedom. Hate can consume us in a wave of bitterness, but whenever we sense the shared core of innocence, we rise on a tide of joy.

We give each activity the meaning it has for *us*. If couples were to consider eating great meals their sacred right, food would become a major problem area. But most couples take good, bad, and mediocre meals in stride—because their purpose in sharing a meal is *larger* than private gratification. Consequently, if your spouse is not a particularly good cook, you usually overlook this. If the two of you have an unexpectedly bad meal at a restaurant, the experience can even be amusing. So why make a mere conversation or the simple act of sex so devastatingly important?

Food critics enjoy very few restaurants; movie critics enjoy very few movies; art critics enjoy very few paintings. Don't become a connoisseur of marriages. Seek instead to be easily pleased.

When they make different calls in a game, referees huddle and quickly get the game moving. They put what's good for the game first. Board members meet and move the business past the problem. They put what's good for the business first. But couples get hopelessly stuck over almost everything. They focus on the rightness of their positions rather than the good of their friendship.

The key to a happy marriage is to say, "Yes, dear." If you can't do that, at least be as kind to your partner as you would be to a total stranger.

We get on the floor and crawl around; we say, "Goo, goo" and we play peek-a-boo. That's *loving* the infant. We don't lose our rights or our identity in the process. We also know from experience that if we identify with our weener dog, we sense what our weener dog wants—but at no time are we in danger of turning *into* a weener dog. When it comes to pets and infants, we understand that love doesn't hurt us or erase us. Seeing this, how can we conceivably think that love becomes a danger when we direct it toward our life partner?

Obviously, loving your partner doesn't mean you automatically fulfill every harmful urge your partner has. Your dog may *want* to eat a dead bird, but if you love your dog, you walk him past the bird. I'm not telling you to put your husband on a leash. I'm saying that love doesn't partici-pate in madness. But make sure it *is* madness.

Pet monkeys tear up the drapes. They swing from light fixtures. They borrow your comb without asking. They eat with their mouths open. They hoot all night. They won't put the toilet seat down. They won't attend the meeting. And they won't turn their socks right-side-out. Now, if there are people who can love a pet monkey, you can love your spouse.

The world has a picture of what every spiritual concept should look like. But spirituality can't be pictured in the world. You can't *act out* oneness on a superficial level. You can't *talk* oneness on a superficial level. You may love all animals, but that doesn't mean you fill your house with every stray cat in the city. You may love your husband, but that doesn't mean you follow him around the house saying "I love you." You may love your wife, but that doesn't mean you apologize a hundred times for each mistake you make. Oneness is a deep act of the heart. It's a silent benediction you fail to give no living thing. If you don't withhold *this* blessing, when there *is* something to do, you will know with peace what it is.

To act appropriately in the present, I must see our kids the way they are this instant. God's glasses are love. Let me put them on *first*—so that I can see at least a little of what God sees.

Magazine articles tend to be pro-active rather than pro-inner change: "When your child does that, you should do this." But if I make a rule about how I am going to react to *anyone*, I turn the rule into a god. From then on I will consult the rule and not the peace of my own heart.

I never want to be afraid to *pause*, touch my stillness, then trust my calm sense of what to do *this* time.

It's simple really. Feed the baby when she's hungry. Stop feeding her when she's not. Put her to bed when she's sleepy. Play with her when she wants to play. Isn't that the way God treats us? Did God, the shepherd, ever say to a sheep, "Hey, sheep, I've got rights too! I'll feed you when I'm good and ready!"?

When I make my separate self the focus of my life, I can't love. I can nurture my child—or my inner child. A choice must be made. Both aims can't be pursued at once because they head in opposite directions. And yet when I put my child first, my inner child basks in the warm light of oneness.

Within the heart of God, giving and receiving occur simultaneously. But within a human relationship, giving comes first.

Parenting isn't walking on my knees wiping up the footprints of a little saint. I am not called to self-immolation, but to joy. When I'm enjoying our children, I instinctively feel the right moment to rein in their activities.

Have as few nos as possible. But do have a few. A small child feels cuddled by a few well-chosen nos.

Every child will try out an unhappy approach to life from time to time. We must be wise and not let this go too far. Don't react impulsively; act from your quiet knowledge of *this* child. You are the advocate for his inner strength. You step in and say no because you see that *now* he can do better. From your intuition and calm perception, you see that he has learned all he can from the mistake and now can use a firm hand to guide him.

Our aim is not to keep our child's ego from getting mad at us—we are not anxiously building a relationship with our child. And certainly we are not building a child. We are gently brushing away the dust from an ancient glory, so that we both may stare in awe at what God has already made.

A horse trainer knows not to hit a horse. A dog trainer knows not to hit a dog. In all honesty, do we really think Jesus wants us to beat our children?

Instead of taking someone else's word on what God wants us to do, what possible harm can come from taking God's hand and simply asking?

As a child, Gayle was required to make her bed, and now she doesn't like to. I was never required to make a bed, and now I like to. Decide nothing about your child because of how you *guess* it will play out in the future. Decide with oneness and peace in the present, and for the present. Jesus didn't even *ask* his disciples not to abandon him—he proved to them they couldn't.

I wouldn't like neighbors coming over and playing with our new car. And I don't like just anyone going through our refrigerator. So why do I think my children should *want* to share their toys with other children? When our kids feel our generosity, we automatically teach them to share—but nothing we say or do will *make* them value what we don't value.

Sibling rivalry is a natural human reaction. Nothing has gone wrong. The old cat might not like the new, younger cat. The old dog might not like the new, younger dog. And I might not like Gayle bringing home a younger man and saying, "Look, dear, here's a new companion for you. He loves the Wildcats too."

Please don't tell your kids that, spiritually, they are "one" or even that they should like each other. And in your heart, never criticize them for their ego clashes. Simply do what you can to ease the points of friction between them and, above all, to protect them. Naturally, you won't succeed perfectly—but you can love them perfectly.

It isn't kind to your children to let your needs build up until you explode. If you need a break, take one. If you need a big break, take one. The harm isn't in taking breaks but in thinking we must get angry or turn against our kids in some other way to *justify* the break.

We teach our children to be kind by being kind ourselves. Eliminating "war toys" and competitive sports is not the answer. Children don't mean the same thing by "Bang! Bang! You're dead!" that we do. In a sense, *they* are more spiritually accurate. When we try to convince kids that exuberance is inappropriate, ambition is false, and all play should make some moral statement, we teach the wrong lesson. There's a time to believe that the world holds limitless promise. There's a time to champion causes. There's even a time to show off and try to fulfill yourself by succeeding over others. When you introduce ideas before their time, you set up resistance and delay your child's inner growth.

It isn't necessary to have running battles with your adolescent over taking out the trash, having good table manners, talking on the phone, and bringing glasses back to the kitchen. If a duty adds to the oneness between you, keep it. If it doesn't, drop it.

Your teenager's *function* is to "turn against" you. Don't take this so personally. It's the leaving-the-nest stage. You are the parent. Relax into your destiny. Your function is never to turn against your teenager.

We must let our children make mistakes *and* we must protect them. That's the balancing act.

The adults of every species but ours understand that their first priority is nurturing and protecting their young. Even a wild cat will do anything to protect her kittens. If she has to change her location to remove them from danger, she will do so. If she has to move ten times, she will do so. Don't make the mistake of thinking, "Kids have to learn to deal with the world." No, they don't. They have to learn to *heal* the world. They have to learn that God is Love. The greatest lesson you can teach your children is that *you* would lay down your life for them. So do it. Lay it down. Today.

Our children can see us. They can't see God. Our function is not to describe God's love or to talk endlessly about it, but to *reflect* it so that it can be seen.

All these questions about "should you be your child's friend or your child's pal or your child's servant" are silly. You *are* your child. God has only one Self, one Being, one Child.

If the mind of your child has one honest thought, the truth will take root in his heart. If the eyes of your child have a single tear, that tear will become a river that will float her back to the divine. Therefore, do not despair for your child.

The only price we pay for accepting another's innocence is that we will accept our own.

We can't be judgmental of someone at work and leave it behind just by leaving work. We can't stay angry at our spouse without soon getting angry at our child. If we look fearfully at one thing, a tinge of anxiety settles over all things. Judgment, anger, and fear are total mindsets. But love is total also.

As we flood our mind with the mind of God, our eyes are made whole and our thoughts begin dancing across the images of the world.

Don't seek to dampen your anxieties by meditating. Don't expect to receive blinding insights. Don't look for miraculous changes. Just sit quietly and listen to the hush of heaven. And as you rise, keep it resounding in your ears.

I have no future and no past. I only have God. And there is no fear in God.

I place great emphasis on emotions, but I know from experience that emotions are always changing. I must not judge my turnings to God by how I feel afterwards. "Now that I have prayed, do I have more confidence? Am I in a good mood? Do I feel less vulnerable?" Those questions are spiritually meaningless. The important question is, "Did I try to embrace the joy of God?"

My ego is all in favor of my spiritual path. It has an agenda: to have an effect in the world—even if the effect is no more than an emotional fix.

Turning to our peaceful mind is an unremarkable process. The shift is not accompanied by strong emotion. It's nice when I experience God's peace and presence consciously. But if on many occasions I receive it only unconsciously, I don't want to waste an instant's thought on that fact. Let me simply continue my spiritual journey and be assured that the light of heaven still shines in me and all about me.

God asks only that I make the effort. When we pray or meditate, we never do so alone. I suspect we are helped in our holy efforts far more than we realize. I must never hesitate to avail myself of the One who is with me. Ask for guidance. Ask for help. Say, "I want to know You today. Show me how."

When I find myself thinking, "Oh, no, I just had another idle thought," I obviously believe that the contents of my mind should *look* a certain way. But that approach is doomed to failure. My little mind can and perpetually does manufacture petty contents. Prayer merely loosens my interest in what the little mind is up to so that my *experience* returns to a natural and permanent happiness.

I tend to think of stillness as the absence of everything I can think of! Or at least the absence of everything but "spiritual" words, images, or emotions. But stillness can't be imposed on the little mind. Stillness is already within me, a truth deep within everyone, and so the aim of meditation should be to let my little mind relax, to let it settle down, to *let* it fade from my attention until I recognize stillness as the shining presence of everything.

Like giggling, stillness is infectious. It is getting caught up *completely* in the laughing mind of God.

Prayer as the practicing of life is transforming, but if it's merely a special activity set apart from ordinary events, prayer does little good. The divine mind is a shared mind. The divine heart is a shared heart. So too are life, light, and joy forever shared. And they are shared with all. Prayer doesn't bring reality to light or to life. It's a simple acknowledgment of who and where we already are. It's a simple breathing in of peaceful certainty—and it can become habitual.

Filled with God, we stand before God and within God. But when we ask what *effect* the prayer is having, we turn our gaze toward chaos, the place where all comparisons reside and where questions seem meaningful.

Listen to the ancient words held within all hearts:

You are not lost, my child. Nor do you beat against the walls of hell. Nor have you been assigned the impossible task of changing unreality into reality. Home is within you. The Kingdom is within you. And I am here. Look down, my child, for I kneel before you and wash your holy feet.

I put my trust in You today.

Lead me to Your arms.

Wash me in Your light.

Fill me with Your quietness.

Show me the irrelevancy of shadows—

of discontents and desires,

of resentments and idle thoughts—

*of everything I think I made of myself
apart from You.*

Hold me and talk to me

*until I see myself as You have seen me always,
until I know myself as You have known me
forever,*

until I find myself where I have never left,

bathed in Your joy, secure in Your love,

at home, at rest, at one with You.

Statistically, anxious drivers may tend to have fewer accidents than indolent drivers. Yet many anxious drivers have accidents. No bodily emotion can protect you. Not even stillness and peace can give you some special immunity. Jesus did not lead a sheltered life. Yet Jesus never traded the peace of God for a statistical probability. It doesn't matter what temporary advantage fear might offer you, it's not worth everything.

The peace of God doesn't mean leaving your doors unlocked, or walking down a dangerous street with hundred dollar bills sticking from your pockets. When we try to test a spiritual truth, we inevitably fail.

Little children can get in big trouble fast because they are not cautious. Teenagers may take unreasonable risks because they aren't afraid. In the world, fearlessness is impractical and peacefulness is irrelevant. Yet I say to you, devote yourself entirely to the peace of God.

Anxiety, suspicion, nervousness, apprehension, and other nagging emotions are like a small, yappy dog. The barking may signal a thing you should pay attention to—an indiscreet subject you are about to speak of, an unwise purchase you are about to make, a threatening environment you should leave—but far more often it is merely a part of the ego's endless static. With the peace of God comes awareness and intuition. These you can safely substitute for any form of fear.

We're afraid because there appears to be no *truth*. Except in the most superficial way, no one can agree on what "the realities" of any situation are or on just where meaning and importance lie. One voter sees a truth about a particular politician, yet to another voter the reverse is true. An obvious truth for one city or nation is not true at all for a neighboring city or nation. Within families, merely *discussing* what is true or important about the smallest of issues can cause deep division. During televised games, not only do fans and commentators disagree about what just happened, but, in addition, each camera angle reveals a different "point of view." And in a trial, a witness will swear in the name of God that he saw something different than another witness. This apparent absence of truth makes "getting at" the truth a world-wide obsession, despite the fact that we feel a nagging doubt about almost any pronouncement we make or hear someone else make.

"Truth" is the ground we walk on, yet it shifts beneath our feet. Countless truths lead to countless fears, and even the nature and value of fear itself is seen in contrasting lights. On one hand, movies and books present the ideal of the wholly fearless person. The main character often is afraid of nothing. Fatty foods, tobacco, natural disasters, serial killers, or a hail of bullets all are of little concern. On the other hand, the media pours forth justifications for countless new fears and sympathetically highlights individuals who are afraid. One researcher reports that fear "sets up" many accidents and illnesses, while another expert says that fear can ameliorate painful recoveries from accidents or operations by "preparing" our minds. And today we hear that fears can act as intuitions that guide us away from danger; yet other voices cry out that fears can be "self-fulfilling" and cause what we fear to happen. No matter what ways we use it, fear provides nothing we can count on *consistently*.

There is no final way to determine what a given fear means or what anyone should do about it. There simply is no God in fear, and therefore no reliable meaning in any form fear may take.

No story can be told about the truth of God. It can't be argued or televised. And witnesses can't prove it exists. Yet the truth of God brings peace instantly. There is only one unchanging truth about anyone and everyone. None are left out-side of the warm assurance and gentle rest it offers, because God's truth is Love.

The truth is true. That is the eternal welcome that awaits us now. Nothing can change our Home. Its brilliance is not diminished by our half-hearted efforts. Forget your mistakes and begin again.

Walk straight into the peace of God. Don't look back. Don't ask if you are there yet. Just keep walking.

We're comfortable worshiping God as long as we can keep our distance. It's like peering through the bars at one of those giant mountain gorillas, who we've read are gentle and friendly, but we're not too sure. So we sing about "how great Thou art" but we're not at ease with the thought of Jesus bathing our feet and hand-feeding us.

The world before you will not be destroyed; it merely will dissolve into your Home.

There is no place to go and nothing to do. The ego hears that ancient truth and thinks, "Oh, I should just sit on a couch." But sitting on a couch is doing something.

God is not a set of opinions that distinguish us from others, a series of rules we are asked to argue, or a faith we must defend. God doesn't need us; God has us. God is the grace that rests gently on our eyes, the presence that keeps our hearts from fear, the welcome we cannot wear out. God doesn't divide us from reality. God *is* reality.

Toward the end of his life, Bill Thetford, one of the two people responsible for *A Course in Miracles*, was approached by a man who ran a large Course group. He said that he and the leader of another group were in disagreement over what a particular passage in the Course meant and would Bill interpret it for them. Bill said, "Tear it out." "What!" said the man. "Tear the page out." Bill repeated. "Nothing should come between you and your brother."

I find that in most counseling sessions, those seeking help don't really want God. They want their partner, their child, their health, their personality, or the circumstances of their lives *changed*. There has always been enormous desire to bring God into the events of the world, to use God to eliminate personal difficulties and brighten our lives. Most religions, spiritual philosophies, and even psychological movements promise a means to individual power and enhancement. We have many terms for God—Universal Intelligence, Divine Law, Cosmic Energy, Governing Principle, and so forth—but always we strive to harness this power to give us a happy world. We want God to turn to us, but we do not want to turn to God.

As I listen to people talk about God's "mysterious ways," I get this image of some huge infant in the sky who has gotten hold of a magic wand and is haphazardly tapping individuals, planes, storm clouds, baseball teams or whatever else catches its fancy. No wonder so many religions are filled with fear.

We tell each other that our minds dictate what our bodies do, but the opposite usually occurs. Throughout the day, we are preoccupied with the body and make our mind its servant: "How does my body feel?" "Is my body in the fastest-moving line?" "How is my body being spoken to?" "Is my body having a bad hair day?" "How much money does my body have?" Naturally, we think God's concern must be the same. We meditate or pray so that our loved ones' bodies or our own body will be "blessed."

Many of us today make a simple mistake in logic. If the world is merely a projection, we reason, whatever is in my "mind" is projected or manifested in the world. This, we say, is the "Higher Law." But once again, we confuse the mind with the body. It should be obvious that all the people and events that swirl around us personally are not a projection of our *separate* mind or single brain. For us to believe that would be a form of arrogance. Our mind is of God, which means that our true mind is a part of Love. But if we equate our mind with our body's brain, we are tempted to use our "mind" to acquire and manipulate on behalf of our body. Jesus sought no advantage for his body, and the effect of his miracles was to set those they touched on the road to God, not on the road to acquisition and favored treatment.

I think my life is a logical puzzle that I have only partly put together, so I spend my time moving around the pieces that don't yet fit. If I can just get these remaining few to work, my life will come together. Yet even as I seem to set one or two more in place, the puzzle itself changes, and I have to begin again.

As I look back on my life, I see that I *never* reached a point at which I said, "Everything is as I want it." Nor do I know anyone who has. Clearly, the ladder we climb has no top. "Search but never find" is the only outcome this approach can have.

Fulfillment or "closure" can't be experienced as a comparison because there are no degrees of closure. Either we feel complete, or there still is something missing.

We enter a room of people taller than we are, and feel short. We enter a room of younger people, and feel old. No matter what prize we hold in our hand today, comparisons snatch it from us tomorrow. We want to keep the world *and* perfect it. But this is impossible. The world has no meaning without differences and comparisons. Without these, a weekend wouldn't have "great weather," a business wouldn't be "profitable," a body wouldn't be "healthy," a mind wouldn't be "wise," and a nation wouldn't be "wealthy." How can there be perfection in all things if all things are measured in degrees? How can there be degrees of beauty but no degrees of ugliness? Degrees of riches but none of poverty? Degrees of love but none of hate?

Perfect change can be sought only in the future—where it is destined to remain.

In time's long string of moments, stretching from one side into the recent and ancient past, and from the other side into the near and distant future, only the moment where we stand shines like the risen sun. Only this moment is eternal and indestructible. Only this moment encompasses everything real in brilliant perfection. God's name is I Am, not I Used To Be, or I'll See You Later. The door to heaven is open to us this holy instant, but at no other time.

God doesn't ask you to have lots of thick, lustrous hair, or to be thin and vibrant, or to be financially savvy and socially adept. God doesn't ask that your spouse be a trophy, that your kids make the honor roll, or that your dwelling have curb appeal. But God does ask you to remember God. God is One and asks you to forgive. God is Love and asks you to be kind. God is Peace and asks you to be harmless. God is Joy and asks you to be happy. God isn't interested in your catalogue of mistakes. God wants you to remember your perfection this instant.

God didn't misplace your e-mail address, so stop asking God to remember you. God knows you and loves you forever and forever and forever. You are God's purpose and treasure, God's one great love. There is nothing on God's mind except you. But have *you* remembered God today?

Because they recognize that their *bodies* are in the present, few people doubt that they themselves live in the present. Yet, as adults, we stand so far back mentally from what we are doing that it's as if mere shadow figures are playing out the event. Our attention is on the decisions we have made about this kind of activity, our judgments of the people involved, or our thoughts about what else we could be doing. Even when we like something, we wonder if it will end too soon. Most adults can't eat a simple meal without worrying whether they have enough—or too much—of this or that on their plate.

In contrast, very young children—even when they don't like what they are doing—are wholly within the activity. They interact with strangers, friends, or old "enemies" with little thought about those classifications. They don't endlessly compare what they are doing to similar past events, and they don't become preoccupied with when it will end. Even if they are tugging on their parent's arm to leave, their minds are completely into the tugging.

Disengage from fantasies about the future and past, and return your mind to the present. But do it gently. Gentleness is the present. Be mindful of what you are doing and stay within the instant—but stay within it happily. The present is potentially happy because it is already filled with God.

At this time, it is now. At midnight tomorrow, it will be now. And at high noon in a thousand years, it will still be now. Learning to respond to now is all there is to learn.

The little mind has its own version of the present and uses fantasies about another time and place to escape from "the present situation." Even within riveting circumstances, the little mind must project into the future to give them meaning. What importance would receiving an honor have if the next day everyone carried on as usual? Thoughts of what might come of this give even our best moments their meaning. Thus, the little mind, needing to relate everything to what happened before and what might happen next, is never wholly engaged. Yet within us is a mind that is always here and now. Bringing our attention back to the present and becoming mindful of the task we're doing can be helpful, but to *immerse* ourselves in now we also must open our awareness to peace and enjoyment. By doing this we begin to see *from* the gentle perspective of Love's presence.

We can't single out parts of a dream to prove we are actually awake. *Dreams prove nothing.* As little kids who are trying to stop wetting their beds quickly discover, it's possible to dream you are awake while still sleeping. But the rays of God do shine through the shadows of the world. This evidence of light must become our treasure. The incidences of separation and attack that are all around us are not worth savoring and storing up. Even the favorable ways our life compares to other people's lives are not reflections of God's oneness. Don't mistake good fortune for spiritual advancement. Savor instead the occasions of forgiveness, laughter, thoughtfulness, happiness, love, and forbearance wherever you find them. Make *these* your inner rallying cry, the thoughts you honor and live for.

We can awaken while dying, but we also can awaken while cleaning the cat sand. Perhaps the most deeply held justification we have for delaying our *complete* commitment to God is our belief that death is somehow transformational, or that God's law will reward our efforts at that time. Thus we can say, "Even though I'm not awake now, the little I do each day will lead to it later." But what sense would it make for Love to wait for your organs to fail before stepping in to bless you? It doesn't matter whether you view reported "near death experiences" scientifically or mystically, now continues to be the only time you can know God. And awareness of God is infinitely rewarding. The ego doesn't fade away merely because the body dies, and the eternal doesn't become more present after death. Why would it? Don't put off heaven. It surrounds you this very instant.

Death has neither spiritual nor unspiritual forms.
The *way* we die is not an indication of how we
lived. Nor do the many illnesses and accidents
we may have before dying mean anything. Don't
look back and ask, "Why did I get sick?" To ask
why is to believe there is meaning outside of
God. Only God is meaningful—and God is now.

There is no governing philosophy behind this
picture of separation we endlessly reexamine.
If the reality doesn't contain Oneness, it doesn't
contain reality.

We can *decide* to turn to God at any time—we
don't first need proof that "life is but a dream."
We already have proof of many unrealities yet
remain convinced that God has little to offer us
this instant. Only the *experience* of God is con-
vincing, and that can be sought without proof.
We have merely to recognize that at present we
still think unreality has something to give us.
For example, our dreams at night are demonstra-
bly unreal, yet as we start to wake from them in
the morning, we often try to control them. We
actually think they hold something we want!
The fantasies we have during the day also are
unreal. Yet time and again we use our minds to
pursue them rather than to pursue awakening.
Don't try to rid your idle thinking of all fantasies
or your sleep of all dreams; merely open your
mind to God's holy peace and let it settle over
all your thoughts.

Look at how far you have come, not how far you have to go. Assessing how often you fail to turn to God is not motivating.

Employing mantras, assuming meditative postures, or closing the eyes and attempting to use the mind in some prescribed manner are not more effective or powerful ways to awaken. Whenever we do even the most mundane chore in gentleness and peace, we are already awake.

We must think and act from love in order to know Love. It's true that the world responds cruelly and insanely to almost everything.

For instance, although it ostentatiously gives lip service to their needs, there is clearly no widespread concern for children, victims, or the powerless. However, we will not experience God if we leave those who make mistakes of *any* kind outside our love. Whether our love takes the form of service, prayer, or donations, we must treat everyone as our sister and brother.

We tend to think of awakening as a single, dramatic event, but it is experienced most often during the small moments when we remember the present and return to our actual nature of kindness and joy. These moments increase and join together as we learn that our divine nature, which is loving, understanding, and happy, links us to everything.

To awaken and to stay awake, turn your mind to the waking state. Over and over, turn your mind to where you are, what you are, and who is with you. That's the whole enchilada.

We are born and immediately start chiseling our gravestone: this is the way we are going to be from now on and it will end up an inscription. Our parents manufacture our body and give us ego patterns and dynamics. This is why our conversations with them often seem to weigh us down and make the world very real. Our parents cement our worldly identity in place, but we will not break free until we see them as wholly innocent and love them with all our heart.

Our worldly identity melts before the dawning light of our spiritual identity. Forgiveness is the window through which this light shines. God is our Mother-Father, yet God is also the Parent of our worldly parents, and their spiritual identity is as brilliant as ours. Forgiveness is merely standing for a moment in God's holy light, where our Self, our parents' Self, and the Self of all living things resides.

We didn't decide on our height or foot size, and we didn't *make* our ego—we merely received it. We are responsible for our personality traits and patterns only in the sense that now they are ours to deal with. But we are not responsible for them in the sense that we made them and now are to blame for them.

Our ego is basically set. No matter how much spiritual progress we make, whenever we fall back into our ego, it's still all there. We never succeeded in perfecting it and never will. Simply take God's hand and soar above the pettiness of your past. Within Love, you were perfect before your "formative years"—and you remain as perfect as Love itself.

I say I want to let go of my past, forgive my parents, and put my childhood behind me. But my worldly identity *comes* from my past. What I really mean is, I want to pick and choose among past experiences—because there are parts of my ego I want free of and parts I want to keep. But I will never let go of my past until I release all of it. If I want to know who I am, I must relinquish my worldly identity.

> *Let all thoughts be still within me.*
> *Let the ego dissolve gently from my mind.*
> *And let me forever be,*
> *Only as You created me.*

Our culture centers on this little blooming period we all go through, and from looking at ads, movies, magazines, sitcoms, and billboards, a stranger to our planet would think humans spend most of their lives at their peak. But we spend most of our lives climbing to it or down from it. We call it our heyday, our prime, our glory years, even our crowning point. And indeed this period can rule our mind even as it rules our society's values. That may be tolerable if you're young and headed toward it, or acceptable if you're in it already, but once you have passed your peak earning potential, your peak value on the romance market, your career peak, and your peak of physical vitality—all of which you will do surprisingly quickly—you may think *you* have peaked. Now, the temptation is to spend your energies getting back up to the peak—which is never entirely possible—or being bitter and depressed at the way life has treated you. Do you want the story of your body or the story of your spiritual journey? Only one will be real to you.

Everything on the body either sticks out or
hangs down. As we grow up, more things stick
out. As we grow old, more things hang down.
Then you reach the point I've reached, where
your parts not only hang down, they try to
jump off. Admittedly, there's a certain fascina-
tion in watching everything abandon ship, but
haven't you seen that movie a thousand times?
It's not like it's going to end differently for you.
What about the story your spirit can tell? The
one about how you released the body and began
to soar?

Not eating little creatures is a higher path than eating them. But it doesn't follow that you should have a running battle with your body over meat. I heard a man say recently that the night before, he had eaten a banana instead of his usual two or three cookies before going to bed. He said it was surprisingly difficult, but because a banana has less sugar he thought this new approach would serve his spiritual path. Actually, it probably won't. The key phrase was "surprisingly difficult." We get into these wars with our bodies and end up putting them between ourselves and God. It's an ancient and honored mistake, found in most spiritual teachings, to make rules of behavior that throw up unnecessary roadblocks. Don't get into pointless wars with the will of your ego because your ego will win—and you will become discouraged. Does anyone truly believe that a banana is more spiritual than a cookie? You could eat a banana every evening for ten years and not feel one bit closer to God.

To be happy is merely to do all things in kindness and peace. But many people find this a hard lesson to learn. They say, "If it's not what you do but how you do it, what about heroin, affairs, battering, and so forth?" You simply are not going to pursue a heroin addiction happily. You are not going to hit your spouse or child happily. The very fact that this even has to be stated indicates that most people are afraid to be happy. They don't want to risk giving up the sense of comfort they derive from repeating their familiar patterns of misery. After all, betraying another can feel empowering and getting revenge can feel fulfilling. It takes courage to practice being a saint, and yet it's a risk worth taking. But remember, you have to *be* a saint, not just present a *picture* of saintliness.

We say, "I love to do this and I love to do that, and I *need* a friend or a partner who can share these things with me." Yet there are those who love being with a damaged child, even though that child can do none of the things other children can. Their love for the child makes them happy. We think our needs are our sources of happiness, but they merely limit our sources. We have so few ways we can be free of misery. Yet we alone place limits on where and how we can enjoy ourselves. Practice having no ego and you will be free.

Look at how many rigid stands I've taken in the past that now I see were mistaken. So how is this new stand different? When I take a stand against another child of God, I split my mind. That doesn't mean, never write a letter to the newspaper, or keep taking the car to an incompetent mechanic. But it does mean, take no stand against that mechanic in my heart.

As your body becomes less flexible, let your mind become more flexible. Loosen up your attitudes. Throw off that heavy coat of righteousness and rigidity. Look lightly on your destiny. Look lightly on the world. There's more to seeing than eyes, more to life than a body.

Why do I defend my opinions?
Am I opinions?

My precious opinions never made anyone happy.

Say what is easily forgotten.
Do what is easily overlooked.
Think what is everlasting.

Awakening is not analyzing the awakening process, or analyzing just what the waking state is, or analyzing the type of mistake that keeps us from awakening. Awakening is simply awakening. Forget this latest dream and quickly turn to God.

There is a time to stop searching for truth and forever changing our minds. There is a time to renounce wise cynicism. There is a time to *choose* what we will believe.

In your life you have believed many things, and most of them have proved wrong. Perhaps you have relied on new movements, old religions, or exotic thought systems; on group meetings, therapies, or cutting-edge psychologies—but, inevitably, they disappointed you. You try to meditate and turn to God, but it seems to have no effect, or only one so slight and temporary that the effort appears pointless. Now, here I am telling you to awake. But here you are having to deal with a world that seems very real and a God that seems very remote, if true at all.

All I can tell you is that the time comes when you must make a leap of faith. You won't get there taking one small, safe, reasonable step after another. That got you to this point, but now you have a decision to make, and this time it has to be permanent. Are you going to believe that you are in God or in a place of no God? In Love or in a place where all creatures die alone? In eternity or in a place where change destroys everything? You can choose what you believe. What you believe will not change the truth, but it will determine if this time you awake.

Your spiritual efforts give you no privileges in the world, and yet you seem locked in the world; and all your pleasures and pains, and all the experiences that are important to you, are in the world. What difference does it make if there is another world, another reality? Why not just deal with what seems real and forget awakening?

Because that is how you have always answered this question. You have played out this tragedy a thousand times before. Yet God does wait for you. And those who have awakened await as well your joyous homecoming. Death isn't the door to this celebration. The efforts you make in the present usher you in. If you will but try a little longer, you will see each attachment to the world, and release them gladly. Once you are no longer conflicted, the sustaining arms of Love will lift you up to light and joy. And this little dream of disaster will fade from your mind, and all who were there will be with you now.

We look at the past and think we understand our life, but our function is not to understand our life.

Don't agonize over every little decision. The past can't tell you anything about what you need to do now.

Never make a decision out of regret of the past. Just take God's hand and decide.

We think self-esteem lies in our accomplishments and that our accomplishments are held safely in the past. We honor the past as the storehouse of our essence—but it is the prison of our soul. The past can't tell us what we are. All it can tell us is what we are *not* this instant.

We look in the mirror and think, "This is not the right face. The right face is the one I had ten years ago." We look at our adolescent and say, "You are not the right child. You should be the child you were when you were nine." We do the same with our sex life, our bank balance, our meditations, our weight, and our career.

The question our culture asks about people's lives is, Did they become someone important? Our culture doesn't ask how often they turned in stillness to God. Stillness leaves no mark on the world. But it does unite all souls in a kiss of peace.

Yes, dying is inconvenient. But I have already lost greater opportunities than the opportunity to get out of bed and walk through the world for one more day. Let me go forth this day and lose no more.

We think our life is going to end in a grand finale. No one else's has, but we think ours will. We believe these daily tasks and strivings are leading to something. They're like strings that some day will come together to form a rope we'll climb to an important and splendid platform. "What did I accomplish today?" we ask ourselves. "What steps did I take toward my goal?" But the true question is, What did we *forgo* doing? Did we withhold judgment? Did we decline to attack?

When in the moment I am either fearing a worse future or excitedly hoping for a better future, my mind dwells not in the peace of God.

I struggle throughout a dream at night to accomplish some little something, but when I wake in the morning, I see that the accomplishment was meaningless. Does that mean I should ignore people and problems? In a dream, if I *ignore* people and problems, I am still reacting to the dream.

Although the evidence of separation before us is an illusion, we must honor everyone and do each task carefully and with affection. When we approach our day carelessly, we abandon God and we abandon who we are.

God cares for you and all living things. To do everything with care is to do everything with light. In this way you bring light into darkness.

Planning and order are not less spiritual than indifference and chaos. Wasting time, wasting money, wasting friendships, will not bring the experience of the divine.

Simplify your life and travel lightly. But don't stop brushing your teeth. Most problems in the world don't have permanent solutions, and a spiritual path won't provide any. So pay your bills and wash under your arms. Your mind is perfectible, but your body and the world are not.

How could scrimping and scrounging be more conducive to dwelling in stillness than a nine-to-five job? Remember, there are no worldly rewards for a spiritual path, and this includes money. Don't throw away your job in the name of relying on God. You don't have a spiritual right to a charmed life. You have a spiritual right to a spiritual life.

Obviously, God didn't create money. It's just strips of paper with funny faces. But the power we give it as a symbol must not be underestimated. We think it represents freedom, status, intelligence, self-esteem, and accomplishment. It is a greater symbol of devotion in marriage than sex. Even people thought to be a little insane are honored if they are very wealthy. And many folks believe that anyone who has accumulated great wealth knows how to solve our nation's problems. Although it's an empty symbol, we must remain aware of the significance that our spouse, children, friends, and we ourselves give money, and use it lovingly, wisely, and in the honor and joy of God.

Our distress over money doesn't come so much from a lack of it as from our belief that it can protect us. And yet, no bank account can be fat enough nor health potion strong enough to protect anyone. The world is a place of fear and danger. You can feel safe, but only in God. As our place in God's heart dawns on us, we see money as one of the world's more amusing preoccupations, and we become more generous with the little of it we have.

The infinite doesn't take form in the finite. The temporal cannot reflect the eternal. Money is wholly and forever irrelevant to your spiritual progress. It indicates nothing about you or your "alignment" with God. Being without it doesn't mean you're a saint; having lots of it doesn't mean your consciousness reflects divine "abundance." Forget your wealth, your poverty, or your rise or fall from either state. That is not your story. You are eternal, spiritual, and beloved. You always were.

Notice that when you try to use your mind to acquire, you always feel anxious. Yet when God is the sole aim of your prayers, you always feel peaceful.

I can't use the truth, but I can be it. When I try to use it, I think of myself as separate from it.

What I believe I am will limit or release my gifts to the world.

As our fear of God lessens, we experience God's nearness and love. We even may feel what is called a "personal relationship" with God. If we have this experience often, the temptation is to think that because we can feel that God loves us, we can *use* this relationship to further our success, just as we use friendships in the world. We think there is probably a course of study that would show us just how to do this—how to live longer, how to look younger, how to be financially successful, how to lower our cholesterol, how to find the ideal partner, and so on. We remember Jesus for precisely this reason—Jesus had *powers* that came from God. Maybe studying Jesus is the course. But to pursue a course requires time, opportunity, and intellect. That leaves many, many people out of the loop. Yet Jesus left no one out of the loop. And Jesus sought *none* of these things. By example, he taught us to put behind us who we are not and remember who we are. His course is to forget all courses and turn to God.

When you pray lay aside thoughts
that peck at the body and dive after souls
fears that give birth to needs
concerns that lay ambush to the future
mistakes that make poison of the past

When you pray lay aside thoughts
of where you are and what you are doing
of your struggle to walk the Chosen Path
even your hopes to leave behind
a few final footsteps in the sand

Then pull from under you
what little ground you still stand on
and fall
like a feather into the hand of God

Rest there so lightly so very very lightly
that when you think about it
(which you will not do!)
you will feel no longer where you end
and God begins

How do we maintain our connection with Love? By making it our only goal.

Our friends the Smiths were in line to renew their driver's licenses when a mother in front of them started verbally abusing her five-year-old. They knew from experience that confronting a parent directly usually makes it worse on the child. But the abuse was so harsh that eventually they gave up their place, went to their car, and spent twenty minutes surrounding the mother and child in light. On another occasion, again at the DMV, a mother was having trouble with a screaming baby. The Smiths introduced themselves as grandparents and volunteered to bounce the baby while the mother finished her business. Although they comforted the child, when they returned her to the mother, no one volunteered to let them back in line. Consequently, they had to come back the next day. Yet to the Smiths—because they were able to maintain their connection with Love—this was a small sacrifice indeed.

If you lose your peace, *break with the situation.* If you need to pray now, pray *now.*

"Oh, but that might be too awkward or too much trouble," we say to ourselves. But if we had diarrhea, we would break with the situation. We would get up from the meeting. We would pull the car off the road. We would put down the phone. We would get out of line. We would excuse ourselves from the dinner table.

It's very simple: All we have to do is make the peace of God as important as we make diarrhea.

If I raise my foot to walk, I have a plan. If I open my mouth to speak, I have a plan. If I load up my fork, I have a plan. Living in the present is focusing on God, but it isn't possible to function in the world without considering the future. The world is *nothing* but past and future. So if writing a will, taking vitamins regularly, or buying insurance makes it easier to focus, then do so.

No matter how small, any daily problem is sufficient to rob us of stillness. Don't wait until you are in the middle of the event to remember stillness. Remember stillness first; go through the problem with stillness; and, afterwards, look only to stillness for the outcome.

Stillness is a baby I carry in my arms. Nothing in the world can tempt me to abandon it.

Stillness is the touch of God's hand, not the absence of physical agitation. Stillness is the peace of God's voice, not the absence of distracting noises. Stillness is the light of God's smile, not the absence of disturbing sights.

Be keenly aware of the world's call to judge, and love more the call of God to come Home.

My little mind is comfortable with judgment, misery, and fear. It is uncomfortable with harmony and serenity. It doesn't even like the words. My little mind tries to add fear to the peace I experience. It whispers, "Isn't there something here you're forgetting?" My little mind believes that peace is dangerous because I am protected by fearful vigilance. But the fact is I have seen countless times that fear protects no one. Not even me.

Judgment creates separation, and fear feeds it.

I go over and over the past, revising it and touching it up—as if I could actually change it. I'm striving for at least a sense of control. Likewise, I rehearse conversations and events that might come up, the same way I tried to revise the old ones. But I never can get the words or pictures to come out right.

I have the same results with my daydreams and dreams at night. Tinker, tinker, tinker. Fuss, fuss, fuss. But it's never quite right. I keep forgetting that the world doesn't work—not even in fantasies!

I use spiritual questions to avoid making a spiritual effort. Fear and confusion arise from my ego, not from truth. Although they seem sincere at the time, my questions rarely reflect an urge to embrace truth. A dream, or even the dreaming process, *can't* be understood until the dreamer begins to wake. So if a question stops my spiritual efforts, I must simply go back to the only thing that will get me the answer, which is returning my thoughts to truth.

In my mind, I keep moving what happens in my life from the credit to the debit column and back again. I can't decide whether an event benefited or hurt me. But in my confusion, it's all the same, because as long as the past preoccupies me, the presence of God means nothing.

Although the past is over and the future hasn't happened, I misuse both within the present. My primary way of dealing with the past is to think about it defensively or to feel guilty. My way of dealing with the future is to fear it or be excited about it. In this way I bring what does not exist into the present.

Don't be afraid to look closely at very painful memories. As you look, see God with you and with everyone else. That is accurate seeing. When you picture God's arms around you, your recall is more complete, more truthful. Your increased honesty allows you to stop remembering yourself as either victim or aggressor. If you see that God was there, the past becomes the present, because God *is* with you always.

We can't change the past, but we can replace it. God was there when it happened and that is the only past we have.

To begin healing the past and defusing the future, merely say, "The past is God with me. The present is God with me. The future is God with me. It is always the same time."

Our culture teaches that guilt is humility and regret is a virtue. But isn't this just spiritual arrogance? Could God be mistaken about any of us? In *true* humility, gaze into the still mirror of peace and see your likeness. Don't be afraid to stare into God's loving eyes and know that you are cherished.

The reason we don't try harder is that we believe we aren't worth the effort. But what if you *were* the child of God? What if you *were* the light of the world? What if you *could* erase all pain and in place of misery and death, bestow the joy of angels? *Then* would you try a little harder to forgive your neighbor and a little longer to remember your birth in the image of God? If your answer is yes, you just ran out of excuses.

My ego stays preoccupied with the world through circular thinking. I make a mistake, then dwell on the mistake, then feel guilty for my new mistake of dwelling, then dwell on my my new mistake, and so forth. "See?" my ego says, "You'll never learn this spiritual stuff." But the only thing to learn is that the ego is a dog chasing its tail.

Don't spend one second *chewing* on a mistake. It's a meatless bone.

When Jesus spoke to Paul on the road to Damascus, Paul had just helped murder Stephen and possibly many other Christians. But Jesus merely said to Paul that the way he had chosen was difficult, and to follow him instead. Jesus didn't discuss Paul's mistakes. Nor did the father of the prodigal son discuss his boy's "sins against heaven." God doesn't dwell on our errors. Do we know better than God what to think about? All *any* mistake requires is correction.

You are God's brilliance and bliss. You are the healing of the world, the herald of God's Kingdom, the coming of heaven's peace. You are worthy of nothing less than happiness without anxiety, welcome without qualification, stillness without interruption, and freedom without limitation. Don't trade everything for the few fleeting gifts that come from thinking you are separate, merely because you believe your shallowness is all there is to you. You did not create yourself.

Because the Kingdom is within you, so too are the beauty and peace of the world you see. The flowers and the snow, the brush of new wings, the soft kiss of a parent, all are kept safely in your heart. Nothing has been taken from you. Not one seedling of promise has perished beneath your footsteps on this earth.

To the ego, the opposite of loneliness is to be near other bodies—as long as they are the right bodies, they are not "too near," and you can come and go as you wish. To the ego, the oneness of God is loneliness, because it can't imagine "one" of anything that isn't framed in space and protected by distance. "I need my space," says the ego. "I need my boundaries."

But you are God's joy, and God's joy unfurls forever. You fill all space and extend an infinite distance beyond that, and still you do not end there. And everywhere you reach, your welcome awaits you and your Home surrounds you. Oh holy child, protected and adored, within God's oneness you are everything *but* lonely, because God is Love.

leaping child
lost in agitation
entranced with hopping
from fading rock to fading rock
avoiding the island of this one perfect
moment immovable
as a star wrapped in heaven

enraged child
ghost of a wolf snapping
at its tail
a circling shadow afraid
to enter this blazing instant
life's inextinguishable flame

sleeping child
caught in a net of images
possessed by the thought of an eagle
sheltered in shell
but lost to the sky where you,
oh heir of God, soar in stillness
if you would but blink your eyes

Rowing Home

When Gayle and I were living in Santa Fe, three young men from Idaho came to visit me. They said they wanted to ask me about *A Course in Miracles*. We met in the patio of The Forge restaurant, and halfway through lunch one of them stood up and said, "I think God has a message for you; I'll go to the bathroom and get it." I smiled matter-of-factly, not knowing how they prayed in Idaho. When the young man came back, he said, "God did have a message. It was 'Row your boat gently down the stream.'"

Two weeks before, Gayle had said to me, "Have you ever considered how spiritual the lyrics to 'Row, row, row your boat' are?" I had not, and told her so, and really didn't give much thought to it later. Now God had my attention.

Row, row, row

We all begin in four-quarter time. We start off
knowing everything is for fun—bedtime, meal-
time, *everything*. True, adults have forgotten that,
but haven't we been told that.a little *child* leads
us Home?

your

Row *your* boat, not someone else's. Why?
Because we're all in the same boat! Heal yourself and you simultaneously offer healing to all
the other passengers.

boat

You are not your boat. You just row it. The body
is a flotation device. Therefore you want to
remain aware of how you treat it and of all those
your rowing touches.

gently

God's little joke. If you're rowing *gently* down
the stream, are *you* really moving the boat? No.

You're just not interfering. But it's important to do *something,* because a gentle occupation keeps your ego gently occupied. Gentleness—which combines peace, love, and harmlessness—is the core of this song and of a spiritual path. Even when you try to row *up* the stream, if you row gently, you still are swept in the right direction.

down

Just lean into your destiny. Don't anticipate. Don't expect. Don't brace yourself. Above all, don't tell the river what *must* be on the shore around the bend. Develop the sense of letting the shore come to you, of letting today's events come to you. In other words, when you stay in the present, you coast.

the stream

The stream knows where to go because the stream is Love. God is carrying you piggyback all the way Home. You don't travel on money, your wits, health, time, good looks, or success. You travel on God.

merrily, merrily, merrily, merrily

Notice that you get four merrilies for every three times you row. That's a 33.3 percent return! A spiritual path is just learning what makes you happy.

life is but a dream

Life is *but* a dream—it's *merely* a dream. If you loathe a dream, or fight it, or worship it, your mind remains locked on it. But when you dream gently, when you *float* in the dream, and when you take the dream as it comes—remembering that your boat is in it but that you are not—then you infuse the dream with many merrilies. Merrilies are the waking state! Thus will you flow into the vast ocean of God's great merriment, where you are free even of rowing, and the smile of God is your smile forever.

Index

The *New York Times* has called Hugh Prather "an American Kahlil Gibran." Although a minister, lecturer and counselor, he is best known for his bestselling books, *Notes to Myself, I Touch the Earth, The Earth Touches Me,* and *Notes on Love and Courage.* He and his wife, Gayle Prather, have been married 32 years. They have spent the past 20 years conducting classes on relationships and parenting, and have co-authored a series of books including *A Book for Couples, Notes to Each Other, I Will Never Leave You,* and *Spiritual Parenting.* He lives in Tucson, Arizona, where he is a resident minister at St. Francis in the Foothills United Methodist Church.

Conari Press, established in 1987, publishes books on topics ranging from spirituality and women's history to sexuality and personal growth. Our main goal is to publish quality books that will make a difference in people's lives—both how we feel about ourselves and how we relate to one another.

Our readers are our most important resource, and we value your input, suggestions, and ideas. We'd love to hear from you—after all, we are publishing books for you!

For a complete catalog or to be added to our mailing list, please contact us at:

CONARI PRESS
2550 Ninth Street, Suite 101
Berkeley, California 94710

800-685-9595   Fax 510-649-7190
e-mail Conaripub@aol.com